Dear Parent:
Your child's love of reading starts here!

Every child learns to read in a different way and at his or her own speed.
You can help your young reader _____ confident
by encouraging his or her own _____ also guide
your child's spiritual development _____ cal values
and Bible stories, like I Can Read ____ published by Zonderkidz. From
books your child reads with you to the first books he or she reads alone,
there are I Can Read! books for every stage of reading:

SHARED READING
Basic language, word repetition, and whimsical
illustrations, ideal for sharing with your emergent reader.

BEGINNING READING
Short sentences, familiar words, and simple concepts for
children eager to read on their own.

READING WITH HELP
Engaging stories, longer sentences, and language play
for developing readers.

READING ALONE
Complex plots, challenging vocabulary, and high-interest
topics for the independent reader.

ADVANCED READING
Short paragraphs, chapters, and exciting themes for the
perfect bridge to chapter books.

I Can Read! books have introduced children to the joy of reading since
1957. Featuring award-winning authors and illustrators and a fabulous
cast of beloved characters, I Can Read! books set the standard for
beginning readers.

A lifetime of discovery begins with the magical words **"I Can Read!"**

*Visit www.icanread.com for information on enriching your child's reading experience.
Visit www.zonderkidz.com for more Zonderkidz I Can Read! titles.*

There is joy in heaven over one sinner
who turns away from sin.
— *Luke 15:12* NIrV

ZONDERKIDZ

The Prodigal Son
Copyright © 2011 by Zondervan
Illustrations © 2011 by Valerie Sokolova

Requests for information should be addressed to:
Zonderkidz, *Grand Rapids, Michigan 49530*

Library of Congress Cataloging-in-Publication Data

Bowman, Crystal.
    The prodigal son / by Crystal Bowman.
        p. cm. — (I can read levels. Level one)
    Illustrated by Valerie Sokolova.
    ISBN 978-0-310-72155-0 (softcover)
    1. Prodigal son (Parable)—Juvenile literature. I. Sokolova, Valerie. II. Title.
BT378.P8B68 2011
226.8'09505—dc22   2010016553

Editor: Mary Hassinger
Art direction: Jody Langley

Printed in China
10 11 12 13 14 15 /SCC/ 10 9 8 7 6 5 4 3 2 1

The Prodigal Son

story by Crystal Bowman
pictures by Valerie Sokolova

Once there was a father

who had two sons.

They lived in a big house.

They always had good food to eat
and nice clothes to wear.

The father loved his sons very much,
and he took good care of them.

He wanted to share all that he had
with his two sons.

But one day the younger son

didn't want to live at home anymore.

"I'm going away," he said.

"Please give me my money."

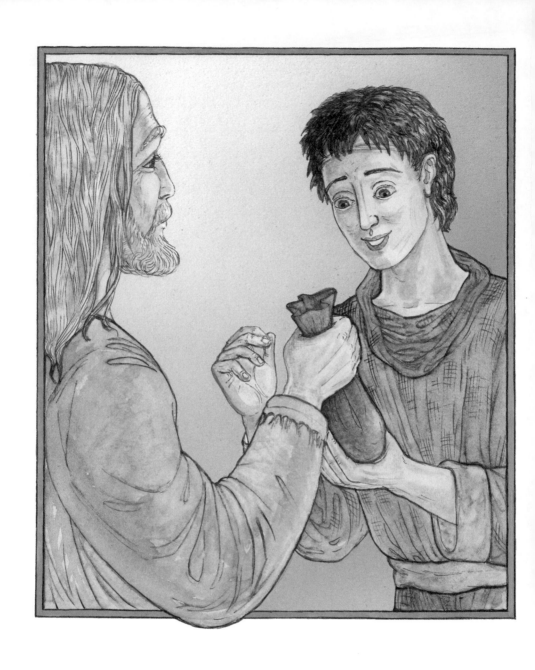

So the dad gave his son some money.

The son went far from home.

He had fun spending his money.

He was happy for a while.

But soon his money was all gone.

The son became hungry and sad.

He got a job feeding some pigs.

But he still did not have

enough money to buy food.

He was so hungry that he had

to eat the pigs' food!

"I know what to do!" he said.

"I will go back home

and tell my father I am sorry.

I will ask my father

if I can work for him.

Then I will have food to eat."

So the son hurried home.

But while he was still far away,

his father saw him coming.

His father was so excited

that he ran to meet his son.

He threw his arms around him

and gave him a kiss.

The son said to his father,

"I have been a bad son.

I should not be called your son."

But the father said,

"We will have a feast and be happy

because you came back home."

The father put a robe on his son.

He put a ring on his finger

and sandals on his feet.

Then he told his helpers

to make a big feast.

The older son was out

working in the fields.

When he came home,

he heard music and dancing.

"What's going on?" he asked.

"Your brother is home,"

said one of the helpers.

"Your father is very happy.

He is having a big feast."

The older brother was not happy.

He did not want to have a feast

for his brother.

"What's wrong?" asked his father.

"Why are you so upset?"

"I work hard for you every day,"
 said the older son.

"I always obey you.
But you never have a feast for me."

"You are my son," said the father.

"You are always with me.

All that I have is always yours.

But your brother was gone

and now he is home.

That is why I am happy."

Jesus told this story to help people

learn more about God.

Jesus said, "God loves us

and takes care of us,

just like the father in the story.

God wants to share all of his

good things with us."

31

Just like the father in
Jesus' story,
God will always
welcome us home.